Understanding Civilizations

Stefan Stevens

INFOMAX COMMON CORE READERS

Rosen Classroom™

New York

Published in 2014 by The Rosen Publishing Group, Inc.
29 East 21st Street, New York, NY 10010

Book Design: Mickey Harmon

Photo Credits: Cover Werner Forman/Contributor/Universal Images Group/Getty Images; pp. 3–24 (ruins) Anton_Ivanov/Shutterstock.com; pp. 3–24 (paper texture) argus/Shutterstock.com; p. 5 Dorling Kindersley/Getty Images; p. 9 Vladislav Gurfinkel/Shutterstock.com; p. 11 Phaitoon Sutunyawatchai/Shutterstock.com; p. 13 (pharaoh) Andrey Burmakin/Shutterstock.com; p. 13 (Chinese statue) The Curious Travelers/Shutterstock.com; p. 15 Ma Lin/Wikipedia.org; p. 17 DEA PICTURE LIBRARY/Contributor/De Agostini/Getty Images; p. 19 (Chinese temple) kajornyot/Shutterstock.com; p. 19 (pyramids) WitR/Shutterstock.com; p. 21 British Library/Robana/Contributor/Hulton Fine Art Collection/Getty Images.

ISBN: 978-1-4777-2619-8
6-pack ISBN: 978-1-4777-2620-4

Manufactured in the United States of America

CPSIA Compliance Information: Batch #CS13RC: For further information contact Rosen Publishing, New York, New York at 1-800-237-9932.

Contents

Ancient Times

People have been around for many thousands of years, but didn't always have organized communities. Life has changed a lot between then and now. Today, we live in towns and cities, and our lives are very modern. What changed in order to get us where we are today? One of the first steps was the rise of civilizations.

"Civilization" is a word used to describe an advanced society with a common government, laws, **religion**, and **culture**. Understanding ancient civilizations is an important part of learning about the past.

There were many groups of people who lived in the past, but they're not all considered civilizations.

By the River

Civilizations didn't just develop, or form, out of nowhere. They formed as people changed their ways of life. The earliest people always moved around. They didn't stay in one place for long. However, over time, they began to settle in areas with many resources, or objects from nature that can be used. They built shelters and grew their own food.

The most important resource was water, so many civilizations developed near rivers. Rivers provided water, food, and rich soil for farming. Civilizations grew as more people moved to these areas.

ANCIENT RIVERS

river	civilization	fun fact
Tigris, Euphrates	Mesopotamia	"Mesopotamia" means "land between two rivers."
Indus	Indus River valley	The Indus River valley refers to many rivers in the Middle East.
Yangtze	Ancient China	The Yangtze has been used for trade for over 2,000 years.
Nile	Ancient Egypt	The Nile River is the world's longest river at 4,160 miles (6,695 km).

The most advanced societies were in China, Egypt, an area of India called the Indus River valley, and an area of the Middle East called Mesopotamia (meh-suh-puh-TAY-mee-uh).

Trading Ideas

Being near rivers not only provided many resources to ancient civilizations, but it also made trading easier. Traders used the rivers, in addition to roads, to travel to different civilizations. This helped spread ideas, goods, and beliefs. As a result, many societies shared the same characteristics although they developed in different parts of the world.

A characteristic is a feature that tells us what something is like. By looking at the characteristics of a civilization, we can see what life was like thousands of years ago.

Today, some of the paths once used for trading in Asia are known as the "Silk Road."

Jobs and Social Order

Before societies formed, people had to know how to do many kinds of tasks to survive. However, once people settled in towns and cities, they were able to **specialize** in one job, which is a characteristic of civilizations. Some people farmed, while others made tools or goods such as **pottery**.

Focusing on one task allowed people to become very good at their work. Their crafts were better and helped make life better for people in society. These improvements helped civilizations become more advanced.

Today, scientists called archaeologists (ahr-kee-AH-luh-jihsts) help us learn about civilizations by studying the objects they left behind.

The specialization of jobs led to another characteristic of civilizations—social classes. Social classes are groups of people who share the same kinds of jobs or same rank in society.

The lowest social class was made up of the poorest people. The next class was made of merchants and artists. Members of the army, called warriors, were above them. The next highest class was made of rich landowners, or nobles. **Priests** were the next highest class. The leaders—such as pharaohs (FEHR-ohz), emperors, kings, and queens—were at the top of society.

Chinese emperor

Egyptian pharaoh

Ancient civilizations had a central government that made the rules for all people. Pharaohs ruled ancient Egypt, while emperors ruled ancient China.

Practicing Beliefs

Priests and rulers were seen as the most important members of society. People believed priests were able to talk to gods, so they were trusted and respected. People also believed the gods chose their leaders, making them the most powerful people in society.

Religion was a big part of ancient life. The gods were said to have control over the weather, crops, and other parts of everyday life. People believed praying to the gods meant they would be taken care of after they died.

King Wu of Zhou

First emperor of the Zhou dynasty (1028–256 B.C.)

Ancient rulers often came from the same families. The Zhou family ruled ancient China for 800 years.

Representing Life and Beliefs

One way people practiced their beliefs was by making art that represented their religion. Art from ancient civilizations was made in the form of pottery, tools, and pictures. For example, one picture might show a god making the crops healthy. A pot could show the story of how a civilization believed the gods created people.

Today, we study art from ancient civilizations to see what was important to the people back then. It's a great way to understand a culture's beliefs.

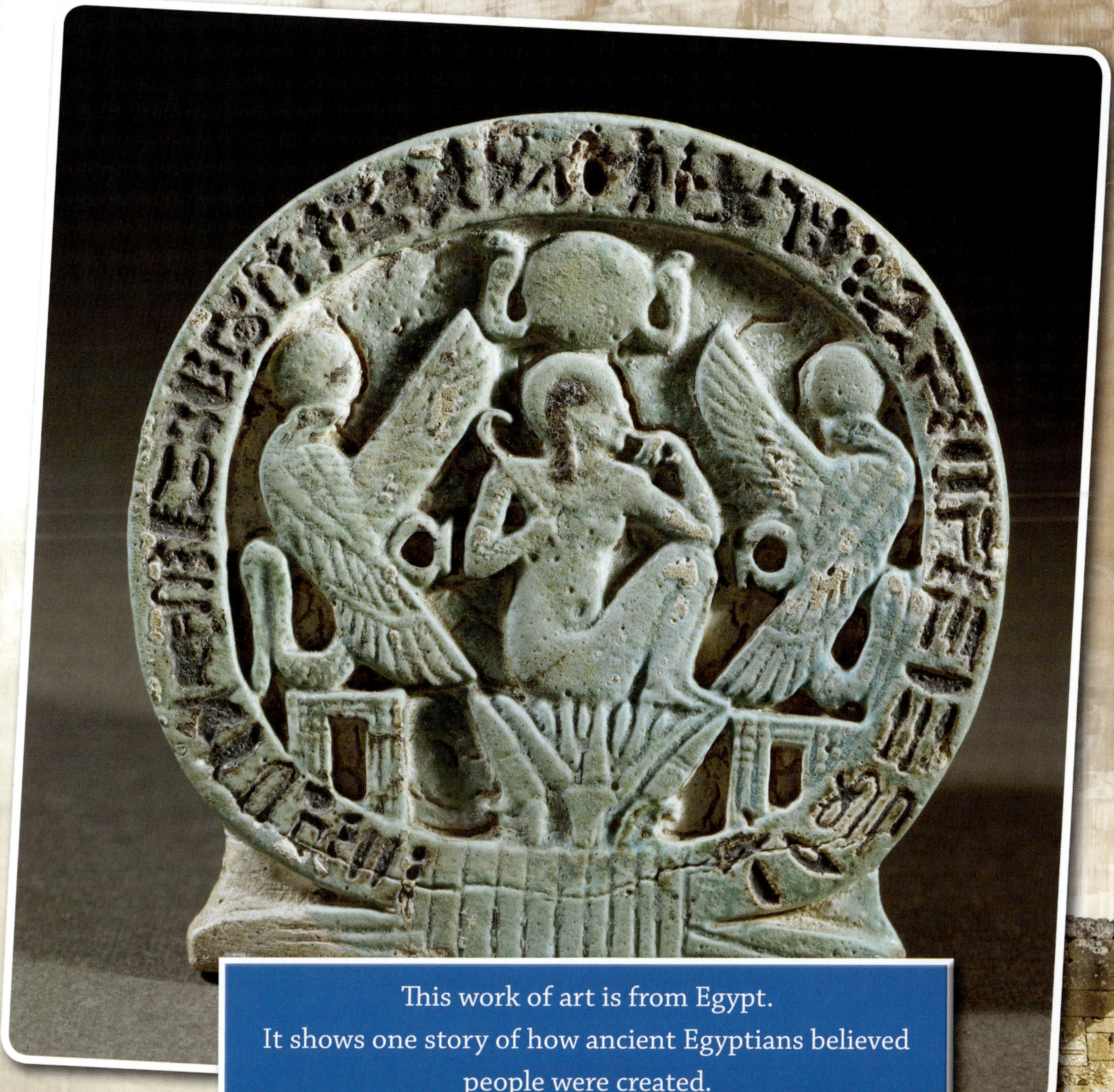

This work of art is from Egypt.
It shows one story of how ancient Egyptians believed people were created.

While some people made art, many people in ancient civilizations worked on roads, buildings, and other public works. These **structures** are an important characteristic of advanced civilizations. They allowed civilizations to grow by making their borders bigger.

In ancient Egypt, laborers made **pyramids** to hold pharaohs' and queens' bodies after they died. Laborers in ancient China built temples as places to pay respect to their gods. These buildings show us that these societies had the skills and tools to build advanced structures.

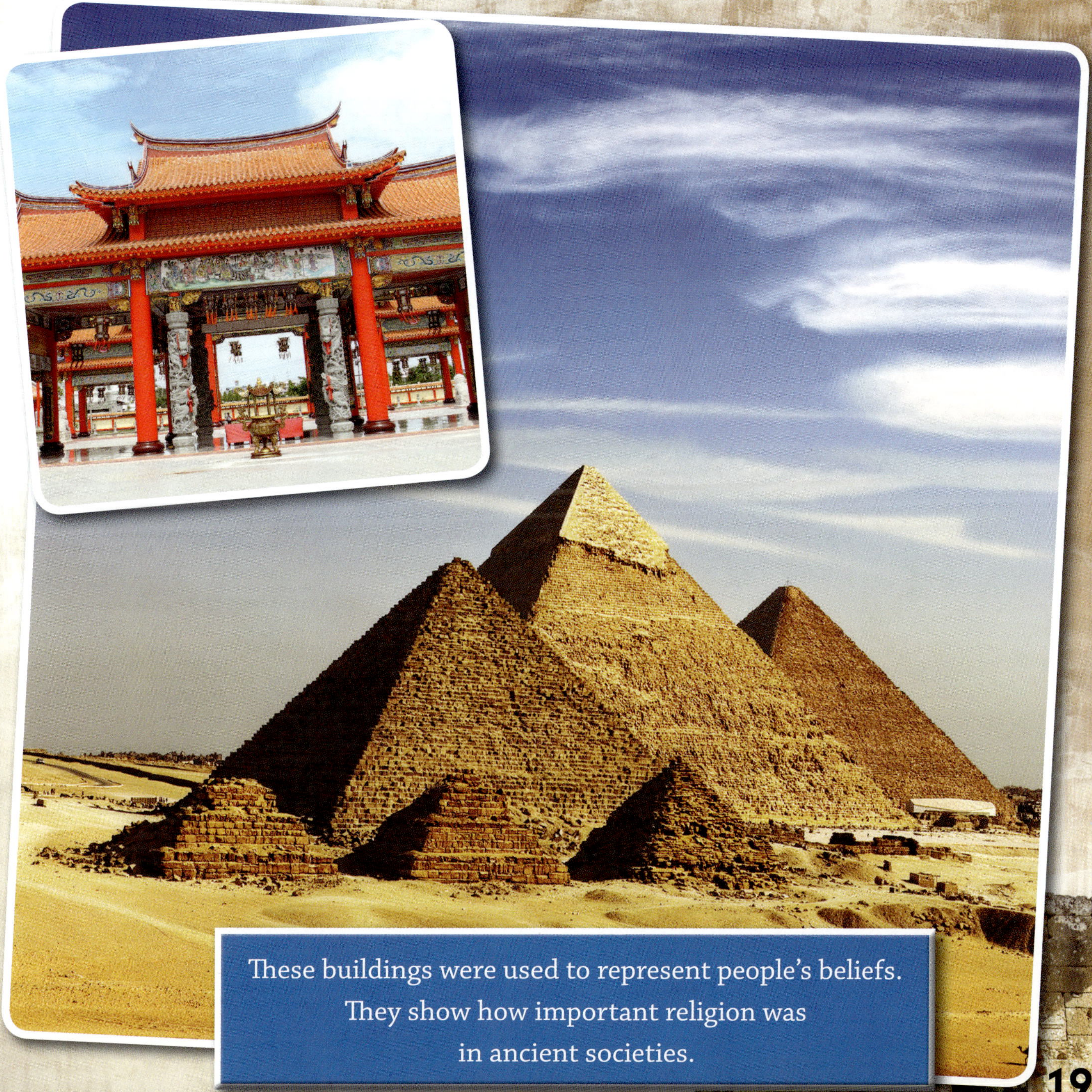

These buildings were used to represent people's beliefs. They show how important religion was in ancient societies.

A civilization's places of worship held many important objects. Most of these objects had writing on them. Early societies each had a system of writing, so that's considered an important characteristic, too.

Writings started off as pictures called glyphs (GLIHFS), which stood for objects or ideas. People drew or pressed these pictures onto wet clay. The writing stayed there after the clay dried. Sometimes, people wrote on animal bones! The writings can teach us a lot about the civilizations.

Ancient Chinese priests used oracle bones like this one to answer questions people had about their lives.

Studying the Past

Ancient civilizations existed thousands of years ago, but the advances in these societies have affected our lives today. Like civilizations of the past, we have a central government, a system of writing, different jobs, and even special buildings. People practice many different religions and make arts and other products, too.

Although they existed all over the world, different civilizations had many characteristics in common. Studying them can teach us a lot about how life used to be and even about how life is today!

Glossary

culture (KUHL-chuhr) The beliefs, customs, art, and ways of life of a group of people.

pottery (PAH-tuh-ree) Pots, dishes, and other objects made of clay.

priest (PREEST) A person who teaches others about religious beliefs.

pyramid (PIHR-uh-mihd) A building with a square base and sloping sides that meet in a point at the top.

religion (rih-LIH-juhn) A set of beliefs about a god or gods.

specialize (SPEH-shuh-lyz) To focus on one task or job.

structure (STRUHK-chuhr) A building or other object that is constructed, or put together.

INDEX